SUSAN JEFFERS

ALL THE PRETTY HORSES

MACMILLAN PUBLISHING CO., INC.

NEW YORK

JE
C. 4

Macmillan Publishing Co., Inc.,
866 Third Avenue, New York, N.Y. 10022
Collier-Macmillan Canada Ltd.

Printed in the United States of America
10 9 8 7 6 5 4 3 2 1

The artwork was prepared as black
pen-and-ink line drawings, with overlays
done in acrylic paint for yellow, gray-blue
and rust. The typeface is Souvenir Light
with the title hand lettered.

Library of Congress Cataloging
in Publication Data
Jeffers, Susan.   All the pretty horses.
[1. Lullabies]   I. Title.   PZ8.3.J393A1   '76
73-19053   ISBN 0-02-747680-4

CL

for my dear friend
Rosemary Wells

Hushaby,
don't you cry.

Go to sleep, little lady.

When you wake, you shall have

all the pretty little horses.

Blacks

and bays,

dapples

and grays.

All the pretty little horses.

Hushaby,

don't you cry.

Go to sleep, little lady.